GRACE UNDER PRESSURE

Early Winter and the Hope of Spring

A Devasting Tragedy Requires Amazing Grace

A story of the Grace of God during Extraordinary Pain

A true story written by Kathleen Mosby

Grace Under Pressure: Early Winter and the Hope of Spring

© 2023 by Kathleen Mosby

Publishing Coach: AdvisedByAmber.com | Advised By Amber, LLC

Printed in the United States of America

ISBN: 979-8-218-21341-1

A Devasting Tragedy Requires Amazing Grace

A story of the Grace of God during Extraordinary Pain

A true story written by Kathleen Mosby

I dedicate this book to my daughters,
Amber and Keisha.
I love you to infinity and beyond!

Acknowledgments

My Parents, without them this wouldn't be possible. My brothers for their love and support. Special shout out to Uncle Norman and Aunt Rita, Bishop Johnny Brice and Elder Glenda Brice without your prayers I wouldn't have made it through the roughest times in my life. Thank you, Harry, for your love I will always cherish our time together it just was too short. Love you always.

Special dedication to my parents Annie and Ishmael McGinnis, Uncle Norman and Aunt Rita Wanger. Bishop Johnny Brice and Elder Glenda Brice. Calvary Ministries in Youngstown, Ohio, NCBC church family in Columbus, Ohio and Higher Praise Worship Center here in Detroit, Michigan along with so many others who have prayed for me.

A very special thank you to my big brother/cousin Matthias Robinson, I listened which I don't always do but this time I heard you! Now the cover is complete for that I say thank you with all my heart. Love always.

Thank you Terrance High for your support and helping me mend my heart and restore my faith in love. Love you.

CONTENTS

Foreword

My life has been filled with highs and lows just as everyone who lives on this planet. I give God all the credit as he has always been there for me not just in the bad times but the good times as well. One of my favorite scriptures is "I know the thoughts that I have for you saith the Lord, thoughts of peace, and not of evil, to give you an expected end" Jeremiah 29:11 KJV. God doesn't want us to hurt but through our pain and tears we see Gods hand guide us to our expected end, one of victory and joy. I am claiming my ending right now in Jesus Name.

I pray for those who read this book to take comfort in knowing Gods got you! He has no favorites, we are all God's children and he loves us and he wants us to reach our expected end.

Be encouraged and trust God.

Grace Under Pressure

Introduction

Writing this book was very painful and therapeutic for me. My life experiences could have never prepared me for what was about to happen. My parents taught me to trust God no matter what happens in your life. In the good and bad times, you have to know that he will be there and will never leave you! All you need to say is Jesus take the wheel, lead and guide me. I am truly lost without you. When I did this, God gave me his grace, mercy, and saw me through the darkest days of my life. I came out triumph!

In reading this book, I share my intimate journal entries that helped me to live through grief. I pray this book will encourage you to stay strong and keep trusting God even in the darkest days of your life.

And if it seems evil unto you to serve the Lord, choose you this day that ye will serve: whether the gods which your fathers served that were on the other side of the flood, or the gods of the Amorites, in whose land ye dwell: but as form me and my house we will serve the Lord.

Joshua 24:15 KJV

The subtitle of my book *Early Winter and Hope of Spring* came to me from God because the winter can be cold, dark, lonely, desolate, and an empty place. Spring however is a time for new growth. The sun is brighter making it warmer and most people are ready to go out to face a new day. I was born on March 20th the official day of spring. A new life came into the world not knowing what to expect from the world or the life I was given. I was always looking for the new things my life because my life had been full of ups and downs. The one thing that kept me going is I never gave up on God. I always kept pressing for a brighter day. My faith hoped that God would make everything in my life okay. Knowing what I know now, it has only been God's mercy that has kept me.

Just as the season changed I arrived just as the deer gave birth to the fawn , just as the daffodil started to peak through the ground and all the other flowers grow in the Spring and other things come alive in the Spring everything is new and fresh after the dreary cold winter has. After the snow has melted and the ground has unthawed to give birth to a new season SPRING! The short days became longer the night less threating but warmer.

My parents welcomed their first baby Kathleen Marie into their lives after 6 years of marriage. They spent years praying for a child, asking for prayer from their pastor and the whole church, who at the time was a small group of Pentecostal believers who knew how to pray. My mother and father had the faith to believe God would answer their prayer – he did just that. My mother did not know she was expecting, until one day she experienced back pains while cooking for the state convention. A lady by the name of Sister Fryson gave my mother the name of her doctor, and she rushed off to see him. Moments after the doctor checked out my mom, they called my father to take my mother to another hospital because they were about to have a baby! Their mustard seed faith was the start of my life.

God has a plan for me he took care of me in my mothers' womb even when I didn't know myself God knew me. He knew what my life would be like because he knows it all. I know God has a plan for me and I am going to walk into his plan after 59 years. I am still looking to God and he is still looking out for me. The Lord heard my cry, and he dried all my tears and calmed all my fears.

Grace Under Pressure

I love spring the best even though it rains and can be gray but I always know the sun will shine again. Hope for me is trusting in God and living on his promise that he will provide no matter what. In deciding to reshare my life's story, I decided to title this relaunch of my book, *Grace Under Pressure*. God will never leave me or forsake me this is my hope in God. As I grow and lean on God, I do feel I should be farther along in my life, but I am not in charge of my life he is. I pray when you are reading this book you see God's love, grace, and mercy. I pray you see how he sends his angles to protect in every situation. I give him praise and glory for my experiences and this journey called life. Do not get me wrong there are times when I still feel sorry for myself and after 17 years, I know God's grace is still sufficient.

Who I am?

Kathleen McGinnis the oldest daughter of Annie and Ishmael McGinnis. I have two brothers but growing up in the McGinnis house hold we always had a lot of children my parents where foster parents for and we all had chores and rules that we had to follow. The one thing I remember the most is cooking with my mother in the kitchen. My mother was known for her cooking and keeping a clean house and her love for the church.

As a family we went to church and did family functions together. As a child I was so spoiled being called the miracle birth and was the only child for eight years. My parents, god parents, and others at the church spoiled me and I got use to the treatment and I must admit I was a bit bratty at times. It can be a good thing and a bad. It was a good thing for me because I got things other kids did not. For instance, my parents put me in a Jewish Community Center in 1968-69 where I was the only black child there. I have very fond memoirs of those times I went on trips with my Aunt Rita. She would stop by our house or call and ask my mother to get me ready as she was on her way. I would go with her to visit her parents. Aunt Bea would send me post cards from New York and other places she traveled to. I was only 5 or 6 then and that made me feel incredibly special. My mom brought me a rabbit coat and hat to match. I was only 7. I had the biggest closet in the house, and it was filled up plus my dressers. My godmother came over and decorated my room all in pink. All this because I was the child everyone prayed for along with my parents. I was loved by so many and I know it and I took it all in.

The only bad part about being spoiled was I expected that from the boyfriend, husband and any male that would be in my life as a mate to do the same. I was a brat, I wanted what I wanted now! How quickly I learned that things didn't happen like that, as I grew up the kid charm I had didn't work anymore. I had to consider other people's feelings and not just my own. I learned to be empathetic to others.

At the age of 8 my world was shaken forever my mom had a baby! My brother was born in 1972. I was not the only child anymore and the focus was on the baby now. My mother and father had another child when I was 2 but Kim was a still born and my mother vowed, she was not going to do that again. I was put on the back burner at least that is how I felt. After all I was only 8 and I really did not understand. I was 10 when my parents became foster parents and in 1974 my youngest brother became my parents son through adoption. Our house was getting full because we had so many children come through our home until 1980 or so my parents stopped. I guess they were getting tried.

I remember this one Christmas we got everything we wanted, and my mom was so spoiled by my dad he brought her a mink hat and a coat with a mink collar and gave her money for her birthday. What a happy time! In my eyes my dad was my King. I wanted to marry a man with all my daddies qualities. On that day back in the late 70's I knew what kind of man I wanted to marry. The following year I was going to Jr. high school, I had to wear dresses and skirts all the time. I had turned 12 and by the Pentecostal rule at our church woman did not wear pants. At that time, I did not have a choice; no pants, no makeup, jewelry, no nothing. Being the kind of kid I was I would not last long without those things.

School Days

Grace Under Pressure

I grew up during a time where schools were segregated. I remember when schools were desegregated and I was no longer able to attend school with friends from my neighborhood. I was bused to a new school in order for the school to meet the requirements of the new law surrounded around segregation. I was scared the first few days it seemed like the other girls did not like me and I did not know why? In my house and church, I learned to be kind to people and share basic respect. JR high was exciting I started wearing jewelry and heels of course I took them off and put them in my book bag so my mom would not seem them, I was finding my own way in life figuring out the things I like and what I didn't like. Things were great that year and my 9th grade year but 10th grade was awful my whole year. Then we had to change high schools in 11th and 12th grade were good again.

I enjoyed going to school because of the new people, new experiences and a new chance to get it right. I went to the Chiffon Career Center for half of the day and school the other half. I made money sewing and I had new clothes all the time. I even made money from sewing for other people. I made my prom dress and graduation dress. The prom was a big fight at my house due to my parent's religious beliefs, but my aunt helped me and of course I made my after-prom outfit and brought my shoes. My date was really kind a total gentleman and we went to the prom, dinner, after prom and the picnic the day after. Graduation Day was here and now the East High Class of 1982 "please stand and receive your diplomas", I will never forget that day. The graduation parties were great and I tried to make them all when my parents gave me the keys to the car and no time to be home. I was simply happy to be out! We still have class reunions I have been to three so far.

Now on to college which were party times for me I hated going to Youngstown State University I wanted to go to the University of

Cincinnati, but my mother wanted me to stay close to home. My best friend Traci and I were planning to be roommates on campus. I was stuck in Youngstown. I ended up moving out of my parents' home at 19. I moved into a one bedroom apartment because I just got tired of rules. Do not stay out late, don't wear pants or makeup so many don't so I asked the question what can I do? Of course, my mom said you're getting smart and I will knock the breath out of you. So, I said its time to be on my own. I had some things in my hope chest that I used for my kitchen, but I went to Goodwill and got all my living room furniture. I took the extra twin bed my mom and dad had in the basement, so I was all set. It was my first place and I worked two jobs.

Life was Good and Bad

I worked at a hotel I enjoyed meeting people and sometimes famous people would check in, I meet Patti LaBelle and Chuck Woolery and my future husband. He said when he saw me he wanted me to be his wife. He never gave up I wasn't ready to date I had just had my heartbroken, but Bobby said give him a chance and I did.

Two years later we were married on May 28th, 1988 and now our life begins. I am a married woman, and it is time to put all that training to work. I know my house will be clean and I know I can cook. These two skills my mom made sure we had down pack. I really did not know what to expect being married to a truck driver, but I would soon find out. We lived in Youngstown, Ohio for 3 years before moving to Columbus, Ohio. Amber our first child was born in Youngstown by the time she was three we moved. I did not know what Columbus would be like for us but I was ready to move and start a new chapter in our lives. The weekend of Easter 1994 we packed up and moved into a brand-new townhome 3 bedrooms and 2 ½ baths. I didn't even see it until I pulled up to the door. Bobby picked it out, I loved it, now we just needed more furniture.

Within 4 years God blessed us to build a brand new home. Now, I was trying to decide if I should do drapes or blinds. I decided to do both as we settled in our home just before Christmas. I told the girls Christmas would be light this year because we brought the house, they were just happy to be in the neighborhood with their friends. I set up my day care once again. The basement was all set up and ready to go. I had three children to follow me and I needed to fill three slots. March came and all three slots were filled. Life was good!

Grace Under Pressure

A few members of the church lived in the area, so we started walking in the evening together. I was happy and Bobby was happy. He felt accomplished. He was providing for his family something he never knew from his father. He only met him twice and he was young, he told me. I guess that is why he drinks so much trying to numb the pain he felt never knowing his father and brothers. Bobby would drink on the weekends when he came home almost a gallon of vodka. I would try to talk to him about the drinking, but he said I had the problem. I did have a problem, I started eating to battle the loneliness I felt after we moved in 1994.

Eating did damage to my body not the whole family. So now we are dealing with my issue of eating to numb my pain and his issue with the alcohol. Sometimes he would make me think I was losing my mind. His words were so hurtful and he allowed his friend to call me all kind of things and that is his friend? Better yet why would my husband allow his friend to talk to me like that. Bobby would bring Porky over to the house and he would spend the night. I did not agree with this but every time I said something it was a huge agreement, all they would do is drink and smoke. For ten years I dealt with his friend coming around. He even allowed him to call me a bitch and he sided with him because I told Porky he should be a man and take care of his family instead of letting the state do it. I was so mad that my husband allowed his friend to call me a bitch.

From then on after that day I had to learn to shut up and don't be around them even though I hated it. I hated he was in my house around my children but to keep the peace I would bring the girls upstairs with me and we would watch a movie until bed time. Before we moved to Columbus Bobby brought Porky to Youngstown and that was a huge fight because he was gone all week then he brings this person with him. I put Amber in the bed and I went to bed she was 6 months old. The next morning I told him if I wanted to be single and raise a child I would have done that. I got ready for church and got Amber dressed and we went to church. Once I came back Bobby had his bags packed and left out the door. For six months we did not live together he was tucked away at his mother's house but he sent money to pay bills and get whatever I needed for Amber. After he came back we never separated again but I wondered about our future and my dreams.

I always dreamed of marrying a business man, having four kids, a five bedroom house with 3 full baths and 2 half baths. I would plan dinner parties and show off my cooking skills to his boss and coworkers. I was living so far from my dream I did not even know myself anymore. But I stayed with my husband until he died, yes my husband died a young man. After Amber was born I decided to rededicate my life I was not turning back from God this time no matter what happens.

We had more children but I had a miscarriage and then we adopted a little 3 year old girl she was very cute and shy at first. I knew she was the one when I saw her picture. I was not concerned about Keisha's issues, her mother used cocaine while pregnant with her. I just saw a child who needed me to help her. Amber was 8 at this time and by the time the adoption would be final Keisha would be 4.

I found a church I really liked and joined in 1995 that was my support system. The girls and I would go every Sunday. My only concern was now we are in Columbus and Porky would be a fixture at our home. God help me! Our family was happy and the girls enjoyed their friends. My house was the Kool-Aid house and we had a fenced back yard so most of the younger kids would play out there. The older kids played in the front where they created a game called curb ball.

One thing for sure, you better be home by the time the streetlights came on. One neighbor had a pool and in the summer all the kids would be over there and some adults. I loved my neighborhood. When our house was being built, I would drive over and pour anointed oil on the land, I was giving God glory for our place before we even moved in. I had enough faith to believe that my dream was going to happen and it did.

All the neighbors got along and if the kids did not, we stayed out of it. That was kids business (lol). After we got our dog Flip he would run up and down the fence wanting to be with the children. I would bring him in the house when the kids would come over, but he was a very friendly dog, but I did not want to take any chances. Life was GOOD and we were a happy family. Bobby and I had our rough times just as any married couple.

When Amber was 6 months old, we had a huge augment he ended up packing his things and moving out for 6 months just before Amber turned 1 he came back home and we stayed together until his death. Yes, I was a widow at an early age. My husband died a young man in 2006 he was only 48 two years shy of 50. I was left to finish raising Amber she was just 15 and Keisha was 11 when she died. Our life went from happy to sad so quickly. Yes, we adopted a bubbly 3 year old cute and shy at first but once she came out of her shell we called her "tigger." That was because she had Attention Deficit Hyperactivity Disorder (ADHD) from the drugs her mother used when she was caring her. I did not care about that I just saw a child who needed love and we had the love to give. Things were good our family was complete I had most of what I dreamed about my life to be.

THANK YOU GOD!!! We were settled- so I thought!

God only has thoughts of good for me I must keep telling myself that. Things looked good on the surface but behind the closed doors is another thing. My husband would say so many hurtful things to me and I did not understand why? I just took it, now I know that mental abuse is abuse! I thought my husband loved me but sometimes I can't tell what he loved the bottle or me. Yes, my husband was an alcoholic. He was not physical when he drinks but he was very verbal. I felt Bobby needed me to stay in his life he said he never knew how to be a husband or father.

He was a great provider for us I mean we would not have been able to build a house if he didn't work. I worked at home, I did daycare in the home for 14 years which we agreed on after Amber was born. Because he was a truck driver and gone most of the week, we did want Amber to be raised by someone other than her parents. That was our choice don't get me wrong I know as a women we have to help our husbands provide in these days and times but God blessed us and I was able to stay home and work. Bobby always said I was his one in a million a song by Larry Graham. Whenever that song would come on I would cry because he had that song played at our wedding, happy times.

The Real Bobby

Robert E. Stultz aka Bobby was born to a single mother, and he told me he only meet his father once or twice. He said he had brothers but didn't remember their names. He said he never wanted to be the type of father he had, he always said he wanted to be with his children and watch them grow up. Bobby changed jobs when we were in Youngstown so he could be with his daughter, Amber was his pride and joy he had every picture in his wallet she ever took. He was sad when he talked about his childhood, he told me the story of working at 8am delivering papers so he could buy some new converse tennis shoes like the other children.

All wasn't bad for Bobby. He talked fondly of his aunt she would care for him when his mother was at work. He always smiled when talking about playing with his cousins. He talked about his uncles and how they taught him how to be a man and provide for the family. He always felt his uncles were his fathers.

Looking back on our life together Bobby became an alcoholic to cover up his pain. He did not know how to fix his life before we meet and he was hurting, I could tell. Some days when we would talk, he would cry on my chest because he said he never had anyone to love him for who he was. He felt people just wanted to use and abuse him. I asked myself, "How can you walk out on a person who has had so many heart aches?" Yes, I had thought about leaving but I thought about what that would do to him as a man. He was already broken and just maybe I would be the one to help him fix it. I talked to him about getting help with the drinking. He denied he had a problem until he lost his job after 18 years of working for the same company. All because he was drunk behind the wheel of an 18-wheeler. At this point I had stopped being a crutch and I had to wake myself up and support my kids. So, I put the focus on them and myself.

How can you help someone who does not want help? I prayed for him as I always did as a wife that was my duty to pray for my family. I took the girls to church on Sundays and other days they were active just as I was in the community and church. I grew up in church and my family was going to do the same. Bobby would come to special events and our marriage enrichment programs. I was happy about that because that gave us together time. Lord knows we needed it.

Before he lost his job, he worked sometimes 6 days a week, but he enjoyed being out on the road. As they say, absence makes the heart grow founder. I did look forward to him coming home and I would try to make coming home a place where he could let the road go and relax. I would plan special events and just time for the two of us but the alcohol was always a factor. I guess I got use to it but I did not like it. Why was I being a victim of mental abuse? I guess it has to do with my childhood, I love my mother, but she could be rather hard on us with her words and actions. I do not blame her now because now I know it was how she was raised by her parents. Maybe I was conditioned to take to take mental abuse if there is such a thing.

Bobby loved me I know but why he chose to mentally abuse his wife I will never understand. I think maybe because that's how he was treated in some crazy way that's how he showed love. I know it sounds crazy for me to even think that way, but could it be true? Bobby never talked to the girls in any way derogatory that I am aware of. Amber and Keisha always wanted to spend time with their dad when he came home. He took time out with them, teaching them how to play chess and other games.

Grace Under Pressure

Family Vacations

The good times in our life included our vacation trips. When we were dating we drove up to Maryland to visit his longtime friend and his wife. One of the two family trips we went on I will always remember: Basye, VA. We had a timeshare and we took a trip over Thanksgiving week. Bobby and the girls loved it, I thought the timeshare was beautiful. Bobby went outside to look at the stars, he enjoyed the outdoors he looked so peaceful and content. After a couple of days relaxing, we drove into D.C. because it was so hard to find a parking space, we just did a drive by of D.C. This was before 9/11. We drove by the Whitehouse, Lincoln Memorial, The Kennedy Center, and other famous attractions. I hated that trip, but I made the best of it because Bobby and the girls enjoyed it so that's all that mattered. I truly wanted my family to have fun.

I really enjoyed our trip to Hilton Head, South Carolina. We rented a beach house with another couple and their children, which made it more enjoyable because the kids had someone other me and their dad to do stuff with. They went swimming, to the beach and ate seafood. We went shopping and had fun in the sun. We took the kids on a dolphin sightseeing cruise. I enjoyed every minute while watching the girls look at the dolphins. They were able to touch them also. The trip ended with lots of family memories and lots of pictures of a great time.

One year we went on a girl scout trip and we took the girls to Hershey in Gettysburg, PA. I went into an uncharted cave it was a great experience. What fun I had with Amber's troop I was looking forward to Keisha's troop trips once they could travel. Those times will always be a fond memory of the good times we had in our marriage. The bad side of this is my husband was acholic and I couldn't help him, and he did not want to seek help.

Now, my focus would be on the children and myself. I had to do it that way to keep myself sane, I prayed for strength. Bobby and I talked about divorce but I really did not want a broken home so I stayed in the marriage. After all our vows were for better or for worse and I wasn't a person to give up. I did think about the effect the alcoholism would have on the children. All I could do was pray and ask for others to pray with me. Things got a little better and Bobby started to come to church, and I was happy that things were getting better.

Bobby had a setback when his uncle died the one who was like a father to him. He cried and cried about his uncle it seemed like he drunk more than ever at this time in his life. I tried to offer words of encouragement, but he did not want to hear it. I was at a total loss so I prayed even more for guidance and strength. During this time we drifted apart a little but I got more involved with my church and the girls activities. He stopped going to church with us and he blamed God for his uncle's death. I would just listen sometimes because he was so negative and so hurtful. I was just there to support him as his wife.

Years went by and he lost his best friend named Porky they had been friends since grade school. Porky couldn't leave the drugs alone, so they finally overtook him and that was another trying time. We survived! I still felt Bobby needed to go to counseling, but he wouldn't hear of it he would always say I needed it more than he did. In some ways he was telling the truth, so I went to therapy to keep my sanity. Life was getting better because I realized some things were out of my control and I could not worry about it. I went on about my daily life caring for the children in the day care and my two children. The years passed by quickly and it seemed like I was just existing and not really living.

The Unthinkable

The reason things happen to some people is a mystery that God only knows. I truly was taken for a setback with this one. My mom died on my birthday on March 20th in 2015. I was on my way to visit her as she just had her other leg amputated. It was a Sunday afternoon and after church I took Amber to a friend's house she, had some homework to do on a joint project. I called the rehabilitation center to let my mommy know I was bringing her favorite dinner City Barbeque and I was going to sit with her while Amber did her project. Just me and my mom as it was 41 years ago.

I still was a big baby so on my way to the rehabilitation center because I could not reach my mom. I called the front desk they said she was not responsive, so I really became worried about her and rushed to get there. Once I got there, I saw the paramedics working on my mom, she had a don't resuscitate order but my brother had it, I thought for sure they had one at the center. She did not want all that she said once my heart stops let me go. They rushed my mom to the hospital I called my brothers and Bobby to let them know what was going on. Once my brother came to the hospital with the paperwork they stopped working on my mom. They pronounced her dead at 5 something that Sunday afternoon. One of the sisters from the church was at the rehabilitation center and she called the church to let them know. One of the Elders came to the hospital to be with us and have prayer.

I lost my dad 3 days before my wedding, 17 years ago and now my mom on my birthday, why is death surrounding what should be happy events for me. What else could happen? The rest of the year went by fast and I kept doing my normal routine. I missed my mom's phone calls. We would talk every day for two and three times a day. I really missed that. As I grew up I started to understand why mommy and daddy did what they did. I was a parent and it all became clear that they just wanted the best for us and they did the best they could every day of their lives. I appreciate them more than ever. I remember my mom going back to school for her high school diploma despite her wheelchair or her having to take dialysis. I guess that is where we get our determination from. Only God can stop us once we put our mind to do something.

We prepared to go to Youngstown for the services. My mom wanted to be buried by my father because she never remarried. Once we got to Youngstown we stayed with my aunt. My mom had already asked her if we could have people come to her home from the church. Mt. Calvary showed up for my mom and even though it had been a long time the older saints never forgot the McGinnis family. Those who remained at the church showed up for our family and Uncle Norman (Bishop Wanger) preached at the funeral. One thing I will never forget that he said that day was that my mom had her legs now and that she was walking around heaven. My brother in his tribute said mommy was calling our dad McGinnis! She would call him once she got to heaven, she was looking for him. Both my parents were gone and we would need to depend on each other now.

At my mom's memorial service we had in Columbus Amber said her grandma inspired her to pursue her education as she watched her grandma go to school. No matter what she set the example for her. We all had to pick up our lives and move on but we never forgot the love of a mother, grandma, sister and daughter. My mom was the strongest woman I knew, if only I could be like her.

Keisha who my mother loved would spend the night at grandma's house and bake cookies, cook, and all the fun things grandparents do. Keisha would ride her bike to my mom's house and call me once she reached her front porch. My mother was the best grandma. I would often tell the kids that was not the woman who raised me! Bill Crosby was right when he said that "grandparents are just old people trying to get to heaven." She sure let them get away with a lot of things we never could do. I guess I will be the same way when I have grandchildren since you aren't responsible for all their care and you can spoil them and send them home. Now, its 2006 and one year after my mom had pasted things were getting back to normal, as normal as things could be after a loss.

My husband had lost his job in Texas and he was getting settled back in trying to find a job in Columbus. It was March another birthday for me, now I am 42 years old. Life should be getting easier but my life was getting harder. I had to put my family on my back and carry them even though I am still grieving on my birthday. I thought about my mother and how happy she was in this picture when she was holding me. I was happy to see another year but her death overshadowed my birthday. I prayed every year would not be like this but this was the first year. Soon it would be our wedding anniversary and I will be thinking about my dad and his death 3 days before our wedding on May 25th, 1988. We were married May 28th, 1988. Once again Uncle Norman and Aunt Rita were there and the Mt. Calvary family.

My dad was a quiet person and very soft spoken. The total opposite of my mom. I guess it is true what they say about opposites do attract. My mom was the oldest of 12 children of Lilly and Beal Hunt and my dad was the only boy of Ishmael and Marie McGinnis he was the 4th child out of 5 siblings. I remember family reunions being a lot of fun. I would see all my cousins on my dad's side at the big banquet, dancing and partying. All my cousins on my dad's side were older so it was fun to hang out with them. Just thinking back on times with my dad helped me grieve.

The last time we drove to a family reunion in Florida in 1987 was the last year I would be a single woman. We packed a van my uncle let us use to go to Ft. Lauderdale. We had my Aunt Nancy, her grandson, and our family this trip I could drive. It was the best trip and I will always remember this trip just like it was yesterday. Family fun memories that will forever be engrained in my mind. The trips I took with my family I pray they remember just as fondly. So they will have stories to tell their children.

One sunny afternoon the kids were playing outside, and the neighborhood was full of joy and sounds of children having fun after school. Keisha often talked to the kids on the other street and they played together a lot. She had a crush on one of the little boys. Our anniversary was around the corner and I did not know what to plan. This would be 18 years as Bobby and I dated for two years before we married so really, we had been together 20 years. A lifetime so it seems, through the good and bad we hung in there to get to this point. Amber was 15 and her 16th birthday was coming soon as well so I am thinking I would give her a party. Every girl wants a 16th birthday party. I thought of planning a swimming party because her birthday is in the summertime. I started to call around to set up the party. I was happy!

One day Keisha started singing *Cooling Water* by the Williams Brothers one of my mother's favorite groups. I just lost it, my mother would get the biggest kick out of her singing that song. So many good memories my mom and I had our battles just as any parent and child but I know we still loved each other. I know my mom would do anything for me and I would do anything for her. I missed my mom so much even though my life was in a good place. You see my mom came to live with us after her first amputation. She stayed with us for over a year then we found her an apartment all on one floor and my youngest brother came to stay with her. So, Keisha and Amber grew close to their grandma and she did to them. So, her death was still fresh as it had only been a year and a couple of months.

On May 30th, 2006 around 3:30 in the morning we were woken up to a loud noise. The smoke alarm went off and I started calling the kids names and our dog Flip. Bobby was at work, so I did not call out his name. Amber knocked on my bedroom door to make sure I was up. In all the chaos she didn't hear me calling her name so we went downstairs and Keisha was not there. I kept calling her name the lights were on and no sign of fire, once I got into the kitchen to get the phone to call 911, I saw the basement door was open. I called for Keisha and she did not answer so I gave the phone to Amber and I went down to check out what was happening in the basement.

As I went down the stairs, I saw Keisha on the floor of the basement I kept calling her name. Once I reached her I shook her but there was no movement from her at all. Then I looked over and I saw Bobby on the floor as I reached him I saw a gun by him and blood running down from his mouth. As I got a closer look the blood was coming from his head. I told Amber to stay upstairs and I ran back upstairs yelling to Amber call the police. I reached the stairs and gapped the phone and I told the operator what happened. She sent the police and the rest of the night we sat in the police cars. They separated us and I called for Amber telling the officer she was all I had now. I knew Bobby and Keisha were dead.

The smoke coming from the basement was from the gunshots. We had not found Flip yet, and I was thinking did he kill the dog too? The gun Bobby used to shoot Keisha and himself caused the smoke alarms to go off, I did not see any blood around Keisha I just thought she slipped on the floor trying to get upstairs. I was crying and trying to talk the operator and making sure Amber was away from the basement steps. Finally, I told the operator what happened. They were dead and the gun was by my husband. I sat in the police car my head was spinning. I kept thinking about where Amber was. I was calling for her and the police officer told me to calm down and he asked me was there anybody I could call. Calm down, I just had lost half of my family how would you feel. I sitting in the car like I was the one who did something. I needed to know what happened.

A few days before Keisha told the neighbor's son her dad was sexually abusing her and she didn't know what to do. The neighbors son told Amber and she told me. I had confronted Keisha and asked her what happened and what did her dad do. She told me he sexually abused her. All I could think was how and when did this happen. I wondered why Keisha told the neighbor and not me. She did just accuse me of pistol whipping her right before my mom died because I would not let her wear her hair down. Everyone that knows me, know I don't like guns and I never wanted to have one in the home because to many kids get hurt with the guns they find at home. Bobby on the other hand said he wanted to protect us if anybody ever came in to rob us.

We had an alarm and that was enough for me. So now, I had to deal with two dead bodies in our basement because my husband killed our daughter and himself. Everything was so unclear because Bobby said Keisha was lying and that he did not do anything. Going back to the day I found out, I called the doctor and she said that they would have to call the hospital and set up an appointment and that someone would be in touch with us. So we were waiting for the call. It was over the Memorial Day weekend and it seemed like we were waiting forever. I was doing what I was told to do. I had told Bobby that we would get through this and be stronger.

I couldn't blame Keisha for anything. I just did not want her to be lying as this was very serious. I told her to tell me the truth and she repeated the story again about the abuse from her dad. How could I say that her dad, her father really tried to rape her? I asked myself would a father rape his child. I know the answer for me was no! My father would never do anything like that to any of his children, no true father would. I was just going crazy because my husband of 18 years, father of our children committed murder and killed himself. Why Bobby? Why?

It was getting to be daylight and the police asked me who can they call and was there some place we could go. The only person I could think of was my neighbor. We went to her house and they told her what happened. Her husband worked for the police department so they knew him and they let us go to their home. I was still wanting to hold Amber and to let her know it was going to be alright. Our separation seemed like hours and the hours seem like forever. We had to be together. The news cameras grew and we went into the neighbor's home. I asked them to call my brother and his family.

The media was relentless trying to get a story. My house was on display for all of Columbus to see and all of Ohio and everywhere else. I cried for days wondering why Bobby why? Why Keisha? She wasn't perfect but nobody is. Now to plan two funerals for your loved ones is unthinkable but it had to be done. I knew Jesus was with me. My neighbor came with me to make the arrangements. I was still in disbelief that I had to plan a funeral for my baby as she was only 11 years old. She had the rest of her life ahead of her. I was hurting.

Keisha's Life and Legacy

Proverbs 22:6 Train up a child in the way he should go: and when he is old, he will not depart from it.

In the summer of 1998 Bobby and I went to meet this bubbly little girl named Keisha she was 3 years old and very shy at first. I fell in love at first sight I wanted to take her home right then and there. She was in a foster home and they lived in the city of Columbus. I just saw a loveable child who needed a family and wanted to be loved she had much to give. I wanted to Keisha to know she would be loved and cared for. I guess I got the outpouring of love from my parents. We took in my youngest brother as an infant straight from the hospital. Keisha was the third child of her parents and her mother was an addict. Her siblings had already been adopted by a relative but when Keisha was put up for adoption they couldn't take her. The state took over after her mother was taking cocaine and it was in Keisha's system at birth. They tried to give her mom a chance, but she could not get it together.

After we went home that day, we decided to move forward with the adoption. We reviewed all the paperwork on her, talked with Amber, and it was final, our family of three would become four. Bobby was excited as he always wanted to help a child who could not help themselves. We added Keisha to the family, it took at least a year for the process to be complete. She came to live with us in August of 1998 and the process started. Keisha was such an adorable, curious, and affectionate child, who was full of energy. We took her to meet the family in Columbus and Youngstown. Everyone was happy we added another addition to the family. Keisha fit right in and she didn't see anyone as strangers. Keisha was an adorable child, very affectionate, and full of energy.

Keisha loved animals, writing, and music. She took full care of our dog Flip, that was her baby. She brushed his teeth and brushed his coat all the time. Sometimes Flip would run from her. He would hide from her but she always knew where to find him. Later we found out that Keisha had **ADHD** which was why we called her tigger from Winnie the Pooh. She bounced all the time. Caring for Flip kept her calm he was her calming grace.

I enrolled Keisha in a Head Start program near our home. She really was settling into the family and we were getting use to her. She had an award winning smile and her charm would light up the room when she walked in. Kisha was in kindergarten and her teacher Mr. Walker played the guitar. She wanted a guitar because she loved it. That's all she would talk about once she came home, so for Christmas we brought her a guitar and she played it all the time. See now that she was 5 years old she could be in girl scouts, dance, t-ball and swimming, she was busy just like her sister. I was that mom who volunteered to be the room mom, planning the parties. I juggled my time between work, home, and the girls. I was busy but I enjoyed every bit of getting to watch my girls grow into young ladies.

One time Keisha had a lead in a music performance when she was in first grade. I remember how excited she was, her performance was wonderful and I was so proud of her. Her dad couldn't be there but when he came home, he heard all about it. One of her many talents was singing, she loved to sing! Keisha also loved to draw and write poems. She wrote a poem that was so thoughtful and it was read in front of her class when she was only 9 years old. At 9 she had so much wisdom and potential only God could have given that to her. To be used to heal people and cause them to think. She was proud of herself, and she had courage to take risk and be herself no matter what people said.

My life by Keisha Stultz

My life is the rushing water:

It is the natures black raven

Who seeks silver treasure throughout the world

My life is my own not to waste but to keep

I am the spring and evening worshiper of God my life is Me!

Another Poem from Keisha (age 6)

Keisha Marie I am an all star

Because I am in the 1st grade, and I love gym

My favorite food is carrots and I love the Buckeyes

My favorite sport is tennis

I would like to be a veterinarian or dog trainer

I wish we could win the war.

A poem from Keisha about music

A Mother's Day Poem from Keisha

Dear Mother,

I thank you for caring about me because you didn't have to take care of me as a child, but you did because you loved me very much.

I appreciate you because you are my mom and you make me feel safe and clam, writing this makes me feel a little sad because my real mom never had the guts to take care of me.

Your Daughter Keisha

After I read the poem she gave me on Mother's Day that year we had a talk about her birth mom. It was my cue to let her know that her birth mother wasn't a bad person, she just had some issues she couldn't handle on her own. I let Keisha know that her home was not a good place for her at that time and it was better for her to be with another family. Keisha was just 10 years old when we had this talk. I never wanted her to hate her birth mom. As she got older, I was going to give her more information if she asked.

The Legacy of Keisha

My plan is to set up a scholarship foundation in honor of Keisha. I want to help other foster children go to college because Keisha started out as foster child. It is important to me to give back to others who need help. I am still working on details for the scholarship and I am planning to set up a mentoring program to empower young girls. Rachel's Daughters would be the name and the vision is to empower young girls in the knowledge of the Lord. To teach girls to keep his commandments and to walk in his ways to serve the community in a positive manner. I

Keisha smiling, as she always did.

want to help impart into someone else the knowledge I have learned.

Proverbs 22:6 "Train up a child in the way he should go and when he is old, he will not depart from it." Amber and I will always remember Keisha for her smile, personality, and love for God as well as animals. She was a very bright young lady and she enjoyed reading. I laugh when I see the Captain Underpants books because that was one of her favorite stories. Keisha helped in the community. She had her issues but overall she was a good person with a heart of gold.

I took her to counseling to help work through the problems she had. Keisha would have been a world changer I am sure of it because of her determination not to let anything get her down. She always wanted to get the most out of life. Keisha hated bananas but she liked banana bread and smoothies with bananas. I sometimes would sneak a banana on her plate with other fruit she would pick around it, I would laugh. She knew what she wanted. I am glad she is at peace. I know my mom and dad are in heaven enjoying their time together with Keisha. I miss that little girl so much I can only dream of what she would be now.

Self-portrait Keisha drew of what she would look like at 25 years old.

Grace Under Pressure

Keisha would be 28. Hard to believe she would be a grown lady on her own in the world. The Veterinarian at the zoo, married lady, a mom, a writer, or musician the world was open with choices. All I can do is dream about what she would be. I dream often of Keisha she is truly unforgettable. I smile thinking about her and the courage she had at a young age of 3 to love the family she did not know, the courage to love no matter what.

Grief: A Process 2X and Forgiveness

The funerals were all done and we were trying to get out life back to normal, whatever that will be. Grief, sadness, tears, anger, guilt, acceptance, and reconstruction were all things I had gone at some point several times a day. Even now I still feel overwhelmed 16 years later. I know everyone deals with grief in their own way and nobody can tell you when one stage of grief should end and how you should feel. I just take things one day at a time and trust God each day.

I don't know if I will ever stop grieving the loss of my dad, mom, husband, and daughter. Grief comes out of nowhere when you least expect. I just roll with whatever the feeling is that day. Some days I can smile when I think of my family and other days I get angry and cry. I have accepted the fact that they will never come back but I can cherish their memory with my thoughts and pictures and even things I have saved from them. When I am sad I look at the pictures of happy times and it brings me joy.

The denial stage I went through was the hardest because I could not believe Bobby murdered Keisha. I am still looking for a reason why. How could he do that to our daughter, why? Then I would get mad knowing he took her life at 11 years old. I know it's wrong to say but I feel he should have just taken his own life and left our daughter to live her life. I was overcome by the shock of the events of May 30, 2006. I couldn't think straight but God allowed me to get up every day to see a new day and for that I am thankful. Even when I wanted to explode and my brain was taken over by suicide I kept the faith. I asked God to help me and guide my steps that day and every day.

Amber needs me and I need her. I pray often that the devil would leave me alone because I am not giving in to his foolishness! I must get over this it's too much for me to bare on my own. I prayed that Jesus would take over my mind because only Jesus can help me. There were times I thought Bobby was on the road and Keisha was at her grandma's house. Even though they are both dead, my mind started playing tricks on me. I'm grateful that I know God to be a mind regulator! He will keep you in perfect peace if you keep your mind stayed on him.

I now feel I can move on, but guilty feelings overtake me. Sometimes I wonder why I was still left here. The easy answer is, God was not ready for me yet and he has an assignment for me to complete. One the day I chose to forgive Bobby, I looked at on old photo and tears started to stream down my face. Forgiveness came for me out of the blue. I had to let go of the madness I was holding on to, after all I had to forgive Bobby for killing Keisha for God to forgive me. Questions will come and go unanswered. Bobby is the only one who can fill in the blanks. I want to be whole again and I want to be able to love again without fear of what if.

On the day of the funeral, I had to be brave. My family, friends and my church family all had my back along with Amber! I had to ask God to take the pain away and the hurt I felt. I was mad because we couldn't have an open casket for Keisha, my pastor at the time thought it would be best to keep it closed with her friends coming. The whole girl scout troop came from both Keisha and Amber's troop so I am glad they could remember Keisha as she was. The whole time I was screaming on the inside, reminding myself that forgiveness is for me but it wasn't time. I had to be strong and set an example for Amber, a Godly example. She still needed my support. I never want her to forget her dad or the memories we had as a family.

A Message to Bobby

Bobby, I loved you with all my heart and I am sorry my love wasn't enough for you to help you heal. After 16 years I do forgive you, I don't understand why but I forgive you. I didn't know how to help. God told me to let it go and stop worrying about the why so on this day, I free myself. Forgiving you will help me to move on from the pain of this ordeal. When you truly forgive, you can be free and open for God to bless you in so many ways. I never knew or grasped the love God had for me but I feel him holding me wiping my tears and whispering you're going to be okay, I got you. As I wipe my tears, I smile. I know now of God's love.

For God so loved the world that he gave his only begotten Son , that whosoever believeth in him should not perish ,but have everlasting life. John 3:16.

I had to make this personal because God loves me. I know God forgives because he lives in me and saved me. He has kept me even when I didn't want to be kept because that's just how much he loves me as his child. He watches over me and protects me. He forgave my sins and he requires us to forgive 70x7. Can we truly forgive that much when someone has hurt you deep to the core? I must find the strength because I want forgiveness too. It is a process as most things in life are, so I finally choose to forgive you Bobby and stop holding on to what happened. I choose to allow God's healing power to overtake me.

I can never forget what happen on May 26, 2006 but forgive and keep it moving. I was keeping myself in a block and running in the square with no sign of stopping. One day I said to myself what are you doing? That's the day I said God help me to forgive Bobby and I forgive you. I forgive you for so many things you were not aware so I gave it all to God. As they say forgive and forget. I choose to do it God's way.

I will remember the laughter, smiles and joy we brought to each other and the bad times which taught us to love each other even more. All 18 years wasn't bad, the birth of our daughter, the house we had built from the ground up and all the trips we took, those are the memories I will treasure. I will say Bobby you should have taken a different route because murder was not the answer.

Courage to Love again

Out of the blue my coworker started talking about her love life and how she enjoyed going online to meet people. She said I should look for love online because it had been very successful for her. I told her that I did not know how to start it and she offered to come over and help me out. She came over and I set up my profile with a recent picture of myself. I started to look at the men and I sent a few likes and waited. About two days later I checked the site and I saw a note from Walter. I knew I would need to find time to date again and I was hesitant because getting to know someone new can be scary. I took a chance and give him my number.

I had another gentleman who wanted to get to know me too and I said yes to him as well. Walter lived in Michigan and the other gentleman was here in Ohio. This time I knew what I wanted and I was not going to back down from that. I wanted my mate to be God fearing with a church home that he was involved in not just a member. My first date was just over coffee the gentleman in Ohio. He was nice but he didn't have the same goals in mind as I did so we just said it was nice to meet you and kept it moving. I could not be in an empty relationship with just sex cause that's all he wanted. So, Walter and I began to talk more and more then we meet in person when he came to Columbus to visit.

Walter and I had a lot in common, we both grown up in a Pentecostal church, so we knew some of the same people. I felt safe with Walter as he was an Elder in the church. He came to visit more and more, then one weekend I went to Detroit to see him and meet his church family. It was everything I thought it would be. I was very impressed and it felt refreshing. As time went on, Walter proposed to me and I said yes. It was a little less than a year after Bobby's death. I was Mrs. Walter Mosby on April 30th 2007. We went to the Luxor in Las Vegas, it was just the two of us. We said our vows and then had dinner at the Hard Rock café. We toured the city as we only had a few days, so we made this our honeymoon as well. Two for one deal so to speak. We came back home to settle in as a married couple.

The apartment I had was a two bedroom, very small kitchen, living room, eating area, and patio. Within a year, we moved into a bigger place, thank God because I was becoming claustrophobic. Once Amber finished school, we were going to move to Detroit. I did not want to move Amber around anymore but she was going to college so it wouldn't affect her that much. In October of 2009 we moved to Detroit. I laughed because I told Walter I will always be a Buckeye fan, he just smiled. After moving, about 1 year later Walter was staying out all night. When I would ask about the money to pay bills, he would get very upset and go into a rage. I was thinking who is this man?

One day I asked him where were you all night and he looked like he was possessed and hit me in the eye. I could not believe it, then he jumped on me and was trying to hit me some more. I kicked him off of me and I got up, he then just left and went to work. After that I did not see him for almost three days. He put some flowers and a card at the door of the apartment. He called me to see if I had got them and I told him yes and that we needed to talk. We meet at the Applebee's and talked. I was not going to be alone with him as I did not feel safe anymore. We went to counseling and things got much better. We still saw each other at church on Sundays until he moved back in our home. We had been married 3 years at this point and I started to second guess my choice to marry Walter so soon after Bobby's death.

I was so lonely and I had to be strong for Amber. I wished that Bobby was here to see our daughter grow and excel in the world. That wasn't going to happen, because he had taken our dreams away. I could not cry over spilled milk. I made the choice to marry Walter and I dealt with it. I was so confused by his actions and I knew he was only human but, why hit me and think its ok I could not understand. A man should never hit a woman and especially an Elder in the church. Should you stay or go, is the question the counselor asked me. I had to think about it and pray. I bought into the dreams he sold me. Was I a fool?

Walter and I stayed married until he left in 2013 just before our anniversary, it would have been 6 years. He left because I did not want to leave my child behind. Walter wanted to move to Texas to start a ministry. I did not want to move that far away from my family after all Walter could flip out on me and I would never be seen again. I just told him no not now if we could wait until Amber got back into school. She was transferring to Ohio State University to finish her degree.

One day I got a call from Walter's job that he passed out at work and they rushed him to the hospital. I left work and went to the hospital. I called my brother so he could get the car Walter was driving. Once I arrived at the hospital and found his room, he looked so bad. They found out he was diabetic and he had to start taking medication. He was apologetic for hitting me and using bad words. I forgave him and told him don't let it happen again and we will be better on from here. After a while things got back to normal. Walter was gaining his strength back and I was making better choices with food for us. I thanked God we could do our daily task as normal without help.

After a while the old Walter came back. He started staying out all night and trying to be abusive. I had enough. Then one day Walter never came back home, I was so happy, mad, and upset. I felt all these emotions because he was full of sh--, no one would believe he was like that. The Elder and organ player they knew was an imposter and con artist. I fell for the lie. I moved too soon after Bobby's death. Everyone was trying to tell me to slow down and take some more time to regroup but my loneliness took over and now, I was getting a divorce. I never wanted to be divorced but I knew God did not want me in a relationship full of lies and mistrust. I moved to Michigan to start over with Walter but he had other plans, I am so thankful the Lord did not lead me to move to Texas with him.

One Saturday we went over to Windsor, Canada just to have something to do. That was one nice thing about living in Detroit, we were just over the bridge from Canada. We went to the casino for dinner and played a few penny slots then headed back home. Once we got to the border patrol they asked Walter about being in Canada a few days ago. I was thinking this is why he was late picking me up from work. Once we cleared the patrol I asked him about where he was spending his time. One thing I have learned about Walter is he can never give a straight answer. I fussed and yelled because I felt used, he never gave me a straight answer. The pastor at the church gave us a used a van and some money to live and sneaking to Canada was what he did with it while I was at work. We were struggling to survive but God had always taken care of me. So Walter leaving would not be so hard after all.

It's so true, God's grace covers you even in your mess. I chose to stay in Michigan because I was working and I really didn't want to move again. After 6 years I was single again. My divorce was not easy, I had to track Walter down and I didn't hear from him until July, he left in April. I told him I wanted to get a divorce and that I was done. I tried to be a good wife to him and that wasn't enough. I told him no man beats his wife and I couldn't do it with him anymore. My life was too valuable to me and I knew my daughter needed me. He tried to convince me to give him another chance but he had already showed me what he was about so I was gone for good.

My divorce took 5 years. When we were married I stuck with Walter through his job loss and his fight for disability. I worked while he just played the organ for the church. I paid the rent in 2010 that was $650 for a 1 bedroom. He was supposed to pay the rest of the bills as long as I sat by him at the computer. I blame myself for moving too fast and not taking time to find out who the real Walter was. I believed my true love would find me and it would not be a joke! I will never give up on love after all God is love.

After a year it happened again, love had found me. I was shopping at the store and I heard this guy say "you are really concentrating on that bottle" I said "are you talking to me?" When I looked up at him he was smiling at me and he said "yes. we are the only two people in this aisle." I smiled and explained why I was reading the label so hard. He gave me his number and told me to call him. I didn't call for two weeks because I wanted to make sure I was ready for a relationship again. No stupid stuff, I couldn't deal with that nor would I. Harry was his name and we talked about life, sports, and our kids. He was very soft spoken and told me he moved to Detroit from Iowa after his mother died, he was the youngest of 12.

In Iowa he stayed with his aunt. He was originally from Louisiana. I told him I thought he was from the south because he had an accent. So we talked and talked for about a month. We went out on our first date, the OJay's where going to perform on the river front downtown. We were going to meet down there so I put on my favorite color purple. I told him that's what I would be wearing. So we met, we both were smiling and ready for a good date. It was so hot and then it rained and my hair was a mess. My makeup all sweated off but we enjoyed each other's company. Even with all the people around with Harry I felt safe and at ease but we still had a long way to go. I had to take Amber back to Ohio for school, so we made plans for the 4th of July to have a barbeque in the park.

I was excited and I had something to look forward to coming back from Ohio. All summer we spent time together when we were not at work. Harry met my cousins at the Labor day bash and we played our annual game of Uno and spades. We did not want to leave each other's company but we both had to go to work. Everybody liked Harry a lot better than Walter which made me feel good about saying yes to our relationship moving forward. I finally said yes to becoming Harry's girlfriend. I told him my story about Bobby and Walter, he understood and we took it nice and slow.

Eventually, Harry did propose and I said yes, it had been two years already and I was ready to be his wife. Harry had a home on the east side of Detroit and he wanted me to start adding my touch so we went to get paint and curtains. He wanted everything to be ready so when I moved in it would be the way I wanted it. He was the perfect one for me and I was blessed he had so much ambition and foresight about the future our future. He told me he owed his cousin $100 that he borrowed when he had to make some car repairs so he had to pay him back the money but they lived together so he wasn't worried about it. The cousin didn't want to move but Harry told him he had to find a place before we got married.

We were busy getting the house fixed and I did not feel comfortable around the cousin. I told Harry my feeling and he said something to him about moving again and it broke out into a fight. The next day Harry went out to the truck for work and his cousin shot him. I got a phone call and rushed to the hospital but I was too late, Harry died without me by his side. This man would help any and every one if he could, he did not meet strangers. He was the sweetest man and I lost him. I kept thinking now what, will I find love? All I wanted is to be happy and content with the rest of my life here on earth.

To Harry, My Love

Harry, I will truly miss you, you were a hard-working guy and you wanted the best for me knowing all the pain I had in my life. You would wipe my tears when I cried and hold me to make me feel safe. I can never forget the fun times and just sitting on the porch drinking coffee on a chilly fall evening. Those were the good times, now once again I must face life without you. God Help Me!

After Harrys death I vowed to stay by myself and get me together. I had some messed up life changing situations more than enough for one person to handle. Harry supported me when I wanted to write my book and get it published. He gave me the push I needed to follow through and get the 1st book published. He would be so proud that I am starting this book over and I have included him in it. So now to find myself!

As I go back over my experiences, I think about what they have taught me. I don't want to believe I am only living to be hurt, I know

God has more for me. I just have to be patient and wait on God to bring my prince to me. I don't want to be alone, life is too hard alone, but I don't want just anybody. I pray that the Lord helps me to be content. *"Not that I speak from want, for I have learned to be content in whatever circumstances I am in." - Philippians 4:11-13*

Years passed at it seemed that love has found me again, his name is Rick. I will say he is a lot like Harry, but I am not comparing the two because everyone is different in their own way. He wants to get married and that's a plus because I don't want to spend the rest of my life dating. I am taking a chance on love and it can be heartbreaking. I've learned enough to know what I don't want and what I can take. I guess I can take a lot because things keep happening to me. God knows my heart and I don't want to be alone. I know God wants me to find happiness and true love. I don't think that is too much to ask. I pray for God to help me wait and for direction from him in matters of my heart. I trust God to provide for me and my needs according to his riches in glory, he will give the angles charge over me. I must trust him.

Job 1: 7-12

[7] And the LORD said unto Satan, Whence comest thou? Then Satan answered the LORD, and said, From going to and fro in the earth, and from walking up and down in it. [8] And the LORD said unto Satan, Hast thou considered my servant Job, that there is none like him in the earth, a perfect and an upright man, one that feareth God, and escheweth evil? [9] Then Satan answered the LORD, and said, Doth Job fear God for nought? [10] Hast not thou made an hedge about him, and about his house, and about all that he hath on every side? thou hast blessed the work of his hands, and his substance is increased in the land. [11] But put forth thine hand now, and touch all that he hath, and he will curse thee to thy face. [12] And the LORD said

unto Satan, Behold, all that he hath is in thy power; only upon himself put not forth thine hand. So Satan went forth from the presence of the LORD.

I wrote these scriptures out because I think the Lord said to Satan test Kathy, she will trust me and have faith. This is how I feel at times because my whole world is turned upside down! I keep the faith and trust in my heavenly father. The love I thought I found in Rick, wasn't it because he's not the one. We broke up after a year and a half of dating. I felt like I was wasting my time. Heartbreak again but I know love is out there for me somewhere I put it into Gods hands.

Moving on to the Next Phase

How we handle the test is up to us, I want to pass my test just like Job a man of great faith. When all was taken and his family were gone, he still trusted God! Sometimes I feel like the modern-day Job. I have lost so much and yet God is still allowing me to live and witness his goodness. Yes, I know how it may look but I would rather have God on my side than any man on this earth. God is good! I still have my good and bad days usually around their birthdays and the holiday season especially Christmas. Amber and I spend as much time together as possible. Amber now has her master's degree in education and she plans to go all the way to get her PH.D.

I am planning to get my 501c3 to set up a fountain in honor of Keisha. I must keep her spirit alive by helping other children. I finished my degree in business management but I do want to go back to school. I need to get this foundation set up first. Amber and I have been talking about a homeless shelter or housing for people. We are letting God guide us. If you are faced with a devastation or traumatic event look to Jesus, seek professional help because there is nothing wrong with getting counseling. You need to know Jesus is the healer and mind regulator. Talking to a professional to sort things out in your life is a good thing, never let anybody tell you different. I seek out help even now after 17 years sometimes.

I pray this book reaches those who feel like they don't have any hope, because God wants us to live a happy life and full life. Nobody said it would be a piece of cake but life with God is a whole lot easier than life without him. I really hope and pray you are encouraged to fight on and let God guide you because he will never lead you wrong. Trust and believe he's got you. After all these years I know with out a doubt that is true. I didn't say doubt would not come but it is up to us to believe God or believe when the devil tries to tell me stuff. I have to tell him to get behind and take that garbage back to the pit from it came. My God has never lost a battle and he never will. My God is mighty and he watches over me.

God you are the supplier of all my needs and wants. I love you Lord.

Made in the USA
Middletown, DE
06 November 2023

41907897R00033